Become a star reader with Caillou!

This three-level reading series is desig[ned for] beginning readers and is based on p[...] The books feature common sight word[...] [...]r. Each book also offers a set number o[...] [...] are noted in bold print and are presented in a picture dictionary in order to reinforce meaning and expand reading vocabulary.

Level 1 — Little Star

For pre-readers to read along

- 125-175 words
- Simple sentences
- Simple vocabulary and common sight words
- Picture dictionary teaching 6 target words

Level 2 — Rising Star

For beginning readers to read with support

- 175-250 words
- Longer sentences
- Limited vocabulary and more sight words
- Picture dictionary teaching 8 target words

Level 3 — Super Star

For improving readers to read on their own or with support

- 250-350 words
- Longer sentences and more complex grammar
- Varied vocabulary and less-common sight words
- Picture dictionary teaching 10 target words

CAILLOU is a registered trademark of Chouette Publishing (1987) Inc.
DHX MEDIA is a registered trademark of DHX Media Ltd.

Text: adaptation by Rebecca Klevberg Moeller
All rights reserved.
Original story written by Marion Johnson, based on the animated series CAILLOU
Illustrations: Eric Sévigny, based on the animated series CAILLOU

The PBS KIDS logo is a registered mark of PBS and is used with permission.

Chouette Publishing would like to thank the Government of Canada and SODEC for their financial support.

Books
Tax Credit

Gestion
SODEC

Bibliothèque et Archives nationales du Québec and Library and Archives Canada cataloguing in publication

Moeller, Rebecca Klevberg
Caillou: old shoes, new shoes
Adaptation of: New shoes.
For children aged 3 and up.
ISBN 978-2-89718-341-7

1. Caillou (Fictitious character) - Juvenile literature. 2. Growth - Juvenile literature. I. Sévigny, Éric. II. Johnson, Marion, 1949-   . New shoes. III. Title. IV. Title: Old shoes, new shoes.

QH511.M63 2016   ̖   j571.8   C2016-940290-8

Printed in China
10 9 8 7 6 5 4 3 2 1 CHO1972 MAY2016

Old Shoes, New Shoes

JE Moell

Moeller, R.
Old shoes, new shoes.

PRICE: $2.94 (jfe/m)

Text: Rebecca Klevberg Moeller, Language Teaching Expert
Illustrations: Eric Sévigny, based on the animated series

chouette

media®
dhx

Caillou comes down the stairs.

"Ow, my **feet**!" Caillou says.

"Uh-oh,"
says Mommy.

"These **shoes** are **old**.
They are too **small**!"

"You need **new shoes**," Mommy
says.

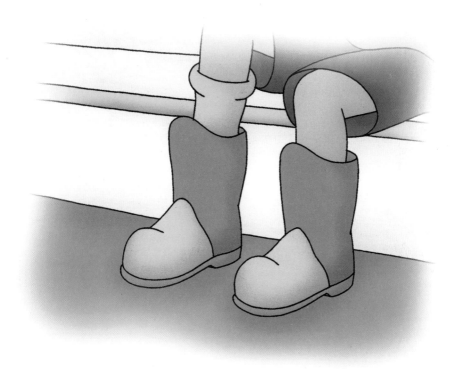

"You can wear these **boots** for now."

Caillou likes **boots** on rainy days.

He can jump in puddles.

But today is sunny. Caillou wants to run and play.

He can not run fast in **boots**!

Caillou sees Sarah.
"Where are you going, Caillou?"

"I'm going to the shoe store. My **shoes** are **old**."

"I need **new shoes**. Then I can run fast!"

"Hooray!" says Sarah. "We can **race**."

Caillou and his mother are at the store. They look at **shoes**.

There are **small shoes**.
There are **big shoes**.

There are running **shoes**, too!
They look fast.

But are they **big** enough?

The man checks Caillou's **feet**.

"Your **feet** are **bigger**, Caillou!" says the man.

"Do you want red **shoes**? Or yellow **shoes**?" asks Mommy.

"I want green **shoes**!" Caillou
says.

Mommy buys **new shoes**, too!

They wear their **new shoes**
home.

Caillou sees Sarah. He wants
to **race**.

"You are too fast!" says Sarah.

Caillou laughs and waves
goodbye.

He can run fast in his **new shoes**.
Caillou is happy.

Picture Dictionary

old

new

small

big

shoes

boots

feet

race